Preface

The Small Book Management Perspective is types of surmise of term of management and its relative terms. It is little and nutshell. Aforesaid book provides proper and specific way to understand the concept regarding management. In the corporate world, it is needed to be familiar with management principles. Lot of books provides in huge and bulky theoretical concept of management. It becomes uneasy to understand. Due to all, the Small Book Management Perspective is put up before the students and business management persons. I hope the small book will give you satisfaction.

Dr. Bharat A. Pagare (M. Com, SET, M.B.A., M. Phil, Ph.D.)
Assistant Professor, Head department of commerce,
Marathwada Shikhan Prasarak Manadals's
Sunderrao Solanke Mahavidyalaya Majalgaon, Beed.

About Author

Dr. Bharat A. Pagare (M. Com, SET, M.B.A., M. Phil, Ph.D.) is assistant professor and head department of commerce at Sunderrao Solanke Mahavidyalaya Majalgaon, Beed. This college is affiliated to Dr. Babasaheb Ambedkar Marathwada University, Aurangabad, Maharashtra state, India. He has more than twelve years teaching experience at education institute of Marathwada Shikshan Prasarak Mandal Aurangabad. The education institute MSPM has 12 senior granted colleges of faculty of commerce. Dr. Bharat Pagare worked 10 years as a head in Vinayakrao Patil Mahavidyalaya, Vaijapur, District Aurangabad. Presently he is working as a head at S.S.M. Majalgaon, Beed. He has written and edited more than ten books. So many national and international papers have been published in difference types of journals. He has worked on so many committees of Dr. B.A.M. University Aurangabad.

Published by
Create space free publication

First Edition: 29 June 2017
Small Book on Management Perspective
Author: Asst. Prof. Dr. Bharat A. Pagare
E mail: bharatpagare47@gmail.com
Typing and Setting: Ashitosh More
Mb: 8275706481

ISBN (10): 1548490741
ISBN (13): 978-1458490744
Author:
Asst. Prof. Dr. Bharat Asaram Pagare
Bhavsingpura, MSEB Road,
Ahinsa Nisarg Colony, Aurangabad

Price: $7

Small Book on Management Perspective

Chapter – 1
Management Concepts

Management means to manage different activities by the people. Management is the activity for getting the work of an enterprise completed through the efforts of other people. It becomes necessary to guide, direct, Co-ordinate and control human efforts towards the fulfillment of certain common goals or purposes. Management represents that skill which directs, regulates and integrates human efforts in the discharge of all operation required for entropies. Management plays a important role in the operation of business enterprise. A business is comprised of several elements viz, Men, Materials, Money, Machines, Methods, Markets and Management. Here has been given seven M's management started at the Top of enterprise pyramid. One has said MANAGEMENT is like a pipeline; the inputs are feeded at the one end and they are processed through management functions like planning, Organizing, Directing and Controlling and ultimately we get the end results or outputs in the form of goods and services, productivity, satisfaction, information, etc.

Definitions of Management:-

1) Koontz O' Donnell :- Management is the task of the manager to establish and maintain an internals environment in which people working together in groups can perform effectively and efficiently towards the attainment of group goals."

2) Peter F. Drucker : - "The first definition of management is that, "It is an economic organ of industrial society. It means taking action to make the desired result to pass."

3) Stanely Vance : - "Management is simply the process of decision making and control over the action of human beings for the express purpose of attaining predetermined goals."

4) Lawrence A. Appley : - "Management is the development of people and not the direction of things..... Management is personal administration."

Management related to planning, organizing, co-ordenating, directing and controlling the human and material resources to achieve the desired goals.

Theo Haimann's Concept of Management

Theo Haimann, in his popular book 'Professional Management-Theory Practice' has
used the word Management in three different senses-
I) As a Noun
II) As a Process
III) As a Discipline

Management as a Noun:-

He says management is a grammatical word as a noun. Management is often used in referring to the group of managerial personnel of an enterprise in the managerial group there are lot of activities, responsibilities having by persons.

Thus, all persons in an industrial enterprise from the managing Director or The General Manager to the first line of supervisor fall under the category of 'Management'.

Management as a Process:-

Secondly, the term 'Management' is also used as away of referring to the process of managing; the process of planning, organizing, staffing, guiding, supervising and controlling. The logic of the management process is that particular functions are performed in a sequence through time. In other words, whatever functions are performed by a manager and the sequence in which they are 'Management Process'.

Ordinary there are two main functions of management, viz,; (i) Decision making and (ii) implementation of the decisions and collectively these two fall under the expression 'Management Process', planning, organizing, actuating, and controlling involved in the achievement of business goals is known as 'Management'

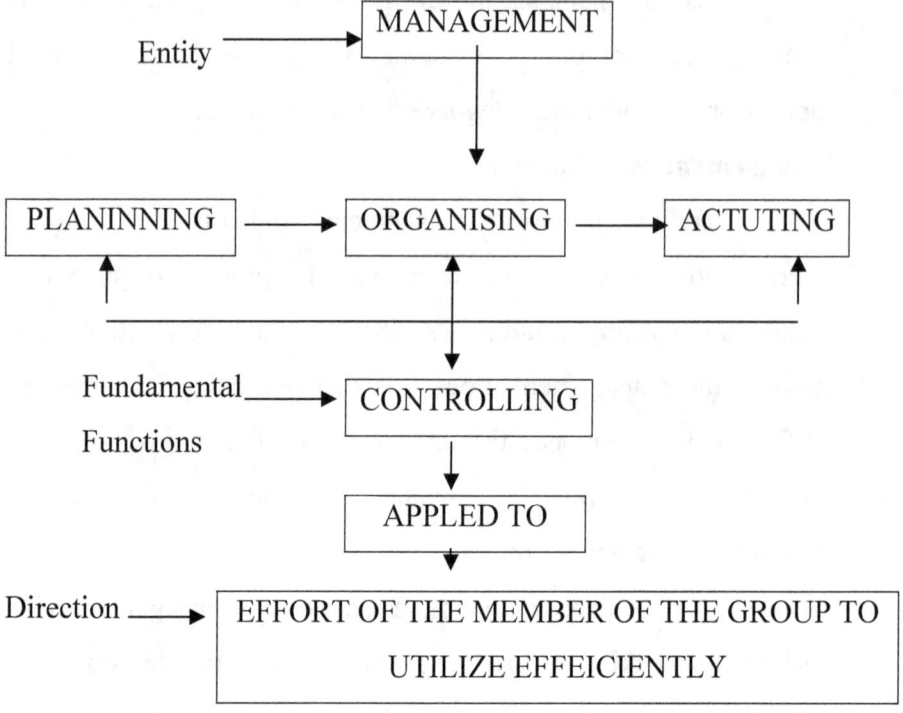

Management as a Discipline:-

Thirdly sometimes the word 'Management' is used to connote neither the activity nor the personnel who exercise it, as a substantive describing the subject the body of knowledge and precise as a whole, discipline, Management has to remain under the discipline; discipline may be as a 'Management' , 'Executives', Or 'Administrators'. Management has a functional concept which is related to best outputs. That comes from sincasity of personal.

Chapter – 2

Functions of Management

There are lots of thinkers in management faculty. They have given differently functions of Management. Let us see functions of management given by top management thinkers.

Henry Fayol:-

The first real thinker of management philosophy and he has classified managerial functions as planning, organizing, directing, co-ordination and controlling.

Luther Gullick:-

He has prepared a list of executive functions under head line of 'PODSCRB'. It has made from first alphabets which is-

P	-	**P**lanning
O	-	**O**rganizing
D	-	**D**irecting
S	-	**S**taffing
C	-	**C**o-Ordination
R	-	**R**eporting
B	-	**B**udgeting

Koontz O' Donnell and Earnest Dale:-

Koontz O' Dannell; Planning, Organizing, Staffing, Directing and Controlling. Besides these functions Earnest Dale treats innovation and representation also as impertinent management functions.

L. Hall:-

According to L. Hall there are five main functions of management.

1) Forecasting II) Planning III) controlling   IV) Motivation and V) Co-Ordination

Massie:

Massie has included the following under management functions, Planning, Organizing, Staffing, Controlling, Communication and Direction.

Niles:-

According to Niles (Mary Cushing Niels) there are four types of functions

I) Organization II) Co-Ordination III) Administration and IV) Leadership.

Gorge R. Terry:-

According to Terry, the functions of management are, I) Planning

II) Organization III) Motivation and IV) Controlling

According above functions given by various thinkers of management we should divided into two categories.

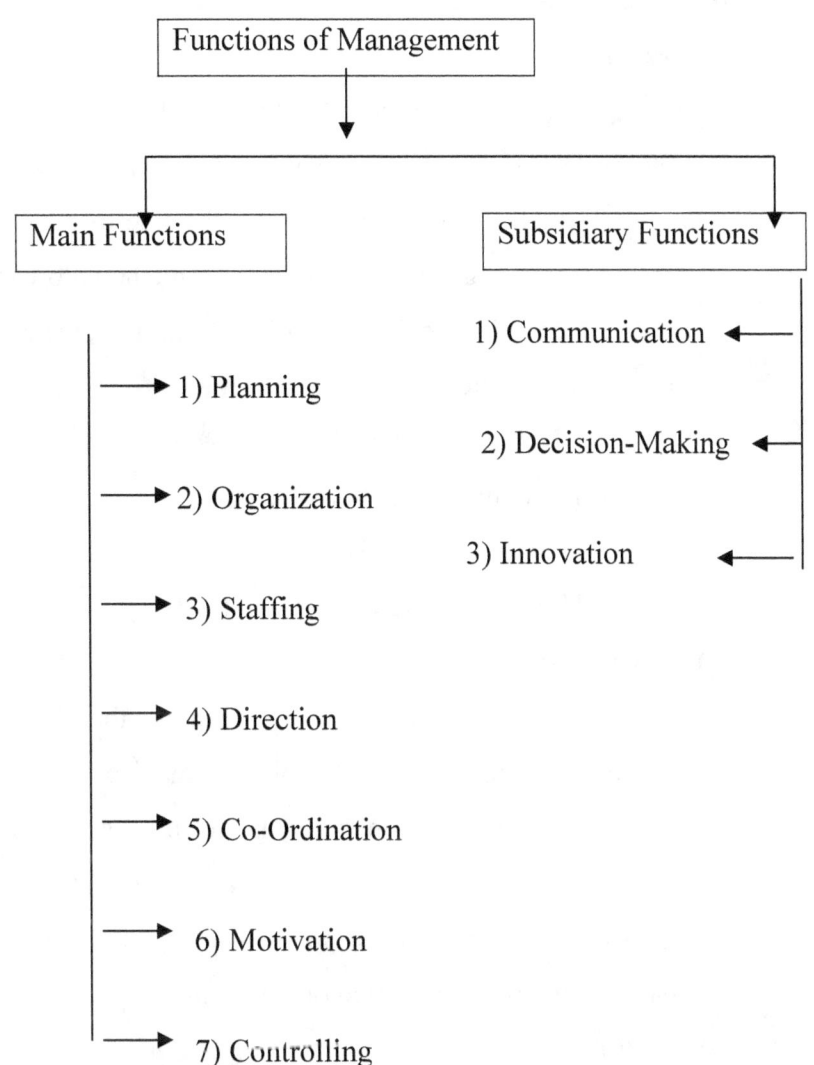

Main Functions:-

1) *Planning: -*

   Planning is related to bright future. According to Henry Fayol, that management should chalk out a plan of action which is the result oriented, the line of action to be followed, to stages to go through and methods to use. It is process of thinking before doing planning creates some question for better future.

   1) What is to be done?

   2) How and where it is to be done?

   3) Who is to do it ?

   4) How results are to be evaluated?

2) *Organization: -*

   After taking decision of planning there must be organization to running the plan. Organization means a group of people. Organization is the process of dividing work into convenient task or plays a vital role in enterprise, their duties in the form of posts, of delegating authority of each so that work is carried out as planned.

3) *Staffing: -*

   Staffing is related to getting good jobber or recruitment. This is process of selection; we have to select candidates who have talent, activity and good personality with sufficient knowledge for positions, fixing financial compensation, training and development, promotion, transfer, etc. Staffing assist in the selection of the right man for the right job.

4) *Direction:-*

Direction is the key to the achievement of the desired result. One is need of directing it gives permission to go ahead. Direction relates to the action one cannot do and go further without directing.

5) *Co-Ordination :-*

Co-Ordination means to give proper guideline to give proper watch, to suggest new solution for created problem. In short Co-ordination among the workers. It aims at canalization of group efforts in the direction of the chosen goals of business. Co-ordination leads to the completion of the production and other function as per planned schedules. Co-ordination develops team spirit and atmosphere of Co-operation among the staff.

6) *Motivation :-*

Motivation means to give inspiration to the related to psychology of workers. It is psychological technique. It's means of triggering human desire to do. Desire and willingness on the part of the workers to perform a given task depends on his attitudes, satisfaction, moral as well as the systems of communication incentive, fair treatment and human approach build-up management.

7) *Controlling :-*

It is a process of observing on staff. Every one has to through plan; one should not go without plan and management. Due to it control must there. Controlling is the final function of management. Due to the proper controlling, result will be as per goal. Therefore Controlling function brings to light the deviations if any and assists the management in making the necessary changes in the plan or policies. That's why controlling gives the tangible result which are related to Business goal.

Subsidiary functions:-

1) *Communication:-*

We have to do communication at the various level of management. We have to present our ideas, Objectives, instructions, suggestions with the help of communication. This exchange of facts, ideas, opinions or emotions by two or more persons is known as communication. It is essential for Co-operation which is the essence of effective management. It provides democratic character to managerial process and strengthens the moral of the people.

2) *Decision Making :-*

It is the most important functions of management. From cradce to grave a manager has to take humorous decisions. Decision making erect awareness of future, it helps in the smooth running of the enterprise. So that decision making has become a pillar of bright future. It is a delegate process, effective process.

3) *Innovation :-*

This subsidiary function relates to research and development, which is essential in this age of competition. All big business-houses have started Research and Development Department to keep pace with modern technique and up-to-date demand.

Chapter – 3
Nature of Management

Management started from human being, but no anyone understood very well about management. There were not arise concept of management. A housewife is a good manager of the family, if she utilizes the resources to the best advantage of the family. Head of the family mat be grandfather, or grandmother may be eldest brother he or she adjust the family with help of own self great experience. Lecturer or lawyer may be called a good manager, if he is able to utilize his time, energy and mental capacities to the best advantage. This kind of activities we know very well present. That's a part of management.

Management – A Class, Team or A Group:-

There are so many faculties and human being had to accept the management by hook or crook. It may be industrial sector, it may be Business group, it may be team of cricket, it may be group of artist. They have own management to be success in every industrial sector there is managerial group which may be classified into three parts-

Patrimonial, Political and Professional. Under patrimonial or family management, the owner become the managers of members of the family occupy key jobs in the management in such classes, the member of the management team do not won their allegiance to the organization, but to the head of the family. This is system is very much popular in India.

Political management is noticeable in Indian public sector organizations; where the political party in power enjoys the rights to manage them. In such cases; the industrial policy is framed by the Government and all top-level appointments are made by it from amongst the political.

In cases of Professional management the management is divorced from ownership. The owners actually provide all the material resources and professional managers look after management.

Life management: -

Life management is part of self development. Human being is a social being. He has to live in society. It has his own life management; such as what to do at the stage of child? What to do at the stage of student life? Which study we have to select? Which way is achievable? After getting achievement what to be done? Which types of obstacles would be creating? Then after he takes a firm decision and settle the self life management.

Management: Science or Art? :-

Management is both a science and an Art. In science there are pacific ways to experiment by the same method, result will be same, and there will not be changes in experiment. We can verify that experiment for many times. And result will be same. May be science described as a systematized body of knowledge pertaining to an area of study and contains some general truths explaining past events or phenomena. Judging from these criteria, it may be observed that management tool is a systemized body of knowledge and its principles have involved on the basis of observation, not necessaries through the use of scientific methods.

Art refers to the way of doing specific things; it indicates how an objective is to be achieved. It is know – how to accomplish a desired concrete result. For example, music is a fine art and perfection. It can be achieved only through continuous practice. From given point of view management is an art and that to a fine art. Management while performing the activities of getting things done by others is required to apply the knowledge of certain understanding principles which are necessary for every fine art. The management gets perfection in the art of managing only through continuous practice, well; the science of management provides certain general principals which can guides the managers in their professional effort. The art of management consist in tacking every situation in an effective manner. The practicing manager can be compared with a carpenter who has to cut refashion and combine the wood of principles to meet specific situations faced by him. In case the present body of knowledge does not provide the solution to his problem, he will endeavor to find out new solution and thus add to the science of management. Infect neither science should be over-emphasized nor art should be discounted. The science and art of management go together hand-in-hand and both are come in existence.

Is management a Profession? :-

The most characteristic feature of modern management is that it is gradually becoming a profession. In yester years, there were only three professions, viz., the profession of bishops, Lawyers and Doctors. In these days of specialization on the other hand, every bread-earning occupation is called a profession. The scope of a profession is not confined merely to Law, medicine and church; nor can every human activity be deemed a profession. A profession is much more than a 'Career' which denotes merely the way of making a livelihood or course of progress adopted by a man is his personal life. A profession is represents a mercantile employment on as a means of livelihood or profit. It is also distinct from 'Occupation' which is merely the means of engaging or occupation. One's time, a profession is an activity which involves earning of a distinct intellectual quality. The term profession may be defined as an occupation for which specialized skills and training are required and the use of these skills is not meant for self satisfaction, but these are used for the larger interests of the society and the success of these skills is measured not in terms of money alone. Thus all professions are occupations in the sense that they provide means of livelihood; however, all occupations are not profession because some of them lack certain characteristics or attributes of profession.

Management is what management dose:-

Let us take an example of money, money is what money does and function four – Medium, Measere, Standard and Store on the same lines it may be said that. "Management is the sum of three different steps involved in it viz,

1) Formation of policy and it's translation into plans.
2) Execution and implementation of plans.
3) Exercising administrative control over the plans.

These three tasks of management may be title as 'Planning', 'Implementing' and 'Controlling.'

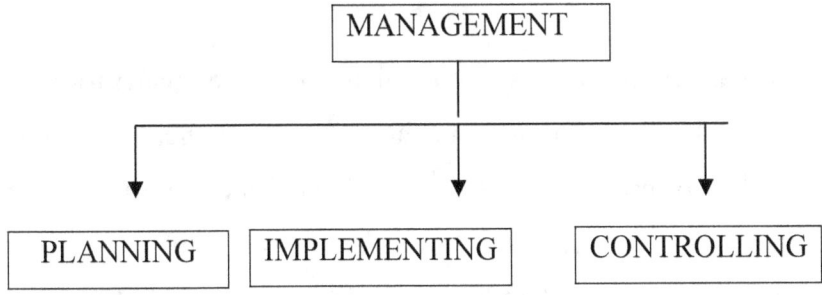

Management is the Development of People:-

Managers do not wait for the future they make the future. Truly speaking, the basic objective of management is to assist the entire organization from top to bottom in bringing about an improvement in knowledge, skill, habits and attitudes that will ultimately express itself productively in work and constructively in human relations. Man-management involves the instituting of an improvement in behavior or potential behavior. There are two important elements which make up the art of management-

1) Human resources.

2) Physical resources.

The term human resources includes personnel administration, training, Development of the natural talents of the people. Development of human personality, etc.

Similarly the term physical resource includes Finance or Money, Raw materials, Buildings, Plant and Machinery and other equipments. The task of management is to manage and administer bohe these resources but human resources is more important compare to physical resources.

Management is a process for the utilization of growth-inputs:-

Resources it may be human and non-human which are related to management. Land and Capital these are the resources include in management and we have to best use of these resources, this think developed because a distinction was made between one who possessed capital and one who utilized it. The enter present may be a person who has his own resources and is also organizing them with a view to attaining economic efficiency and returns or may be a person who does not own the resources but as a custodian of the same organizes it with a view to attaining maximum output and efficiency with minimum input. Management is the art and science of preparing organizing and directing human effort applied to control the forces and utilize the materials of nature fore the benefit of man.

Land, labor and capital with the help of three we have to achieve final goal. Labor is one of them that have feeling, emotion. Management has to motivate them come up slandered of entrepreneurship or industry. Land and capital is there labor is creative part of the organization along with labor factor management remain conscious in progress.

Management is the art of getting things done:-

'Getting things alone' is an art of management. It means to get tasks and activities carried out. It implies that management is not mere philosophy but highly performance-oriented function. Management gets things done through people viz., members of the organization, comprising of both managers and non-mangers. A manager, whatever is his level in the organization, has to get things done through his subordinates. At higher level, the subordinates are themselves mostly manager, it means management of mangers.

Marketing Management	Financial Management	Sale & Advertisement
H. R. Management	**Management**	Customer
Purchase Department	Online Management	Product

Various departments in including in the management every department have itself manager. Such as four departments and it have one manager who is ruing the department, every manager keeps the observation in our department. Therefore the skills which are required to get things done through people include conceptual skills, technical skills, administrative skills, social skills and so on. In order to get things done through people, management has to plan the things which are to be done. So people are creative part in management he has skills, knowledge and can do best.

Chapter- 4
Management versus Administration

What is Management? :-

Management is the activity for getting things done through other people. For getting the work of an enterprise completed through the effort of other people, it becomes necessary to guide, direct, co-ordinate and control human efforts towards the fulfillment of certain common goals or purposes. Management represents that skill which directs, regulates and integrates human efforts in the discharge of all operation required for an enterprise. Management means a combination of some activates which are planning, organizing, staffing, co-ordinating, directing, controlling, and popularly speaking. Management is taken to mean the persons who assume the function of management. But in reality it is a functional concept and doses not include the persons who practice management. Management plays a important role in the operation of business enterprises. A business in comprised of several elements, viz.; Men, Materials, Money, Machines, Method, Markets and Management. Of these seven M's management stands at the apex of the enterprise pyramid and it determines and controls all other factors of business operation. Administration determines the goal and management strives towards it.

What is Administration? :-
Definitions:-

'Administration' is fundamentally the direction of affairs. It is purposive action and to increasing standard of enterprise.

'Administration' is total of Planning, Organizing, Coordinating, Motivating, Controlling and Operating work.

Administration concentrates on the coordination of finance, production and distribution.

Administration frames the policies and makes the necessary adjustment. In business firms, administration refers to the higher and policy-determining levels. Administration is concerned with the determination of overall corporate objectives, policies and master strategies. Its origin is found in the bureaucratic structure of government or from some laws. In government circles, administration is frequently used in the same sense as management is used in private business. In law also, administrators are appointed to look after the estate of a deceased person. Government business administrators while administrating and managing business affairs are to execute the plans and policies formulated by the government.

Top Level

Middle or lower Level

THINKING FUNCTION	DOING FUNCTION

A
D
M
I
S
T
R
A
T
I
O
N

M
A
N
A
G
E
M
E
N
T

Basis of Distinction	Administration	Management
1) Policy Making.	Administration is concerned with policy-making; it determines the goals or the targets to be achieved.	Management is concerned with the implementation of the policy; it is not directly concerned with the goal or target-fixation.
2) Implementation of policies.	Administration is not directly concerned with the implementation of policies.	Implementation of policies framed by administration is the main task of management.
3) Determinative Vs Executive functions.	Its functions are legislative and largely determinative.	Its. Functions are executive and largely governing.
4) Direction of human efforts.	It is not actively concerned with the direction of human efforts in the execution of the plan or policy.	It is mainly concerned with the direction of human efforts in the execution of the plan and policy.
5) Main functions.	Planning and organizing functions are involved in it.	Motivating and controlling functions are involved in it.

6) *Managerial Level.*	It relates to apex or Top level management. Personnel of the top-level like the owners or the board of Directors in charge of it.	It relates to middle and lower level management. Personnel below the top-level like General Manager or Managing Director are in charge of it.
7) *Men Boss relation.*	Administration is the master of industry, which provides the various agents of production and in lieu of this service, earns profit.	Management is the servant of administration; it gets salary or a part of the profit in lieu of its services.
8) *C0-ordination & Control.*	Administration Co-ordinates finance, production and distribution, it frames the organizational structure and exercises control over the enterprise.	It uses organization for the achievement of the targets fixed by administration.
9) *Administrative Vs. Technical ability.*	It needs administrative rather than technical ability.	Management requires technical ability more than administrative ability.

10) Expansion of functions	Its functions expand at the upper level and decrease in importance at the lower laves.	Its functions contract at the upper level and expand at the lower levels.

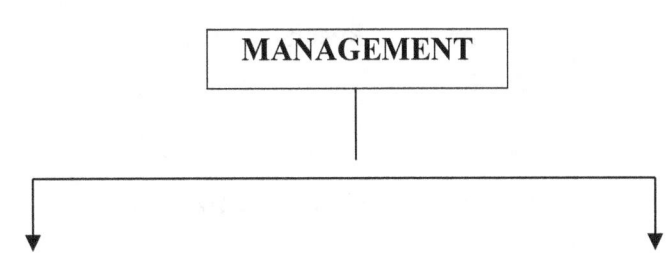

MANAGEMENT

Administrative Management
Management
[Top Management]
lower Management]
1) Policy-Making

2) Policy-Amendment Materials.
and Money
3) Planning
execution
4) Determination of standards
5) Overall control and supervision
control.

Operative

[Middle and

1) Use of
Men, Material,
Machines

2) Policy-

3) Direction
4) Routine

Chapter – 5

Management by...............

There are main seven concepts in management. These seven concepts for getting results through people.

1) Management By Communication (M.B.C.)

2) Management By System (M.B.S.)

3) Management By Results (M.B.R)

4) Management By Participation (M.B.P.)

5) Management By Motivation (M.B.M.)

6) Management By Objectives (M.B.O.)

7) Management By Exception (M.B.E.)

Let us discuss on concepts of management-

1) Management by Communication (M.B.C.) :-

Communication means to give information and to take information. It is a double way process to understanding. Communication is also process of passing information and understanding from one person to another. There are two main types of communication one is verbal communication second is written communication; these are important in business communication, since managing is getting things done. Through others, it is an obvious requirement that the manager must communicate with the members of his organization. It has been estimated that a manager spends 90% of his time in communication, either sending or receiving information. Communication is not a one-way street; it is continuous and coordinated process of telling, listening and understanding.

Information without understanding is an ineffective communication. The success of all managerial functions depends on successful communication. But while communicating, there are lot of obstacles in it; such as not proper listening, not good understanding. What he says? Lack of communication skills.

2) Management By System (M.B.S.):-

System is a way on that we have to walk and go to desire place, with the help of system. But it is related to system, which types of system we accept. The difference between systematic management and traditional management lies in the manner in which decisions are made. The management by system briefly is summarized as :

I) Recognize the problem analyze it and define objective.

II) Gather and analyze the necessary data.

III) Synthesize possible alternatives.

IV) Review and evaluate each alternative.

V) Test conclusions, if possible.

VI) Take selected action.

VII) Review results and if necessary, correct action.

VIII) Formulate and test principals based on experimental results of many cases.

In short management by system is a philosophy of management.

3) Management By Results (M.B.R):-

Results comes from our activities, it may be related to hard work for study, hard work for best products, hard work for constructing buildings; but only hard work is not help to get final result. Systematic hard work, the thesis of this concept's that management in industry deals broadly with control, with getting the work done through coordinating the co-operative efforts of people who have been properly organize into working groups, for the accomplishment of specified purposes.

4) Management By Participation (M.B.P.):-

Participation means involvement in work. How much involvement in work? It decides the good or bad participation, we accepted democracy. So that we strikes, morecnus, bands is it good to participation in the firm; defiantly not, but we have to pay attention to slandered of living which kind of satisfaction they want? Management will have to find out it for that made up a philosophy, that is ………

1) Belief in the doctrine of trusteeship.
2) Recognition that employee is not merely a means of production, but above all human being first and always.
3) Relation that as an employer one is more of a 'Giver' and less a 'Taker' and
4) That worker does not 'Want' money they need money. Once these basic principles are accepted by the employers, workers, instead of treating them as a hostile group or exploiters, under participative management, the board of decision-makers includes the representatives of investors, workers, consumer as also government.

5) Management by Motivation (M.B.M.):-

Motivation relates to moral thing of workers also will to work. It seeks to know the motives for work and to find out ways and means, by which their realization can be helped and encouraged. Motivation gives the tangible result in management. Motivations promote the workers to do work very well with hard work. According to *E.F.L. Breach*,

"The problem of motivation is the key to management in action; and in its executive form. It is among the Chief tasks of the General Manager. We may safely lie it down that the tone of an organization is a reflection of the motivation from the top." General Manager have a decision making power to promote the wormers.

6) Management by Objectives (M.B.O.):-

Some examples of objectives.

I) Salesmen to getting lot of customers and introduced them of our product.

II) For all factory departmental Managers to achieve a given level of output and a budget of expenditure.

Essential steps for Objective:-

1) The establishment of the objectives of the organization as a whole for both the long as well as the short-term.

2) The establishment of long term and short term objectives for each manager clarifying the key results and performance standards he must organization objectives.

3) Periodic performances review of the manager's work by his superior to measure and discuss progress towards results set forth in his statement of objectives.

4) Counseling each manager by his superior to overcome his weakness to build on his strengths and to accept responsibility for self development.

Chapter – 6

Levels of Management

To be for the convenience of study, the level of management may be classified into three groups.

1) Top Management.

2) Middle Management.

3) Lower Management.

Top Management:-

Three important constituents of Top Management.

1) Shareholders.

2) Board of Directors.

3) Chief Executive.

Functions of Top Management:-

1) Determine objectives :-

To determine objective is main function of Top Management. It relates to types of activities, Specialty in work ship, Competitive pricing, Marketing Methods, Widening the area of sales, Relation with the workers, Customers (public), Government etc.

2) To make Policies or Plan :-

It's related to production policy, Marketing Policy, Personnel Policy, Financial Policy.

3) Build up organizational framework.

4) To assemble the different resources; it may be men, machines, capital, land, materials.

5) To control the operation through the organization.

Middle Management:-

This level of management is concerned with the task of implementing the policies and plans chalk out by Top management.

Functions of Middle Management:-

1) To Co-operate in making a smoothly functioning organization.

2) To Co-ordinate in department.

3) To follow the instruction given by Top level management.

4) To build up a company spirit.

5) To motivate the workers to do best.

6) To development leaders for the future by broad training and experience.

Lower Management:-

It is also known as Supervisory Management. This level of management represents the workers before the higher management and the higher echelons of management to the workers. The workers look to the supervisor for orders, policies, instructions pay and so on.

Functions of Lower or Supervisors Management:-

1) To maintain good human relation.

2) To solve the problem of workers.

3) To provide on-the –job training to the workers.

4) To give proper guideline the workers about work procedure.

5) To give orders and instructions to the workers and supervise and control their functioning.

6) To advise middle management about working environment.

7) To arrange for the necessary equipment, materials, tools etc. for the workers.

The Manager & his job:-

The duties of the manager can be defined in a nut-shell as, "To decide what has to be done, to tell somebody to do it, to listen to reasons and get the work done." Manager is a person who gets things done through and with the people in formally organized groups. The manager is the key-man in the organization pyramid. His job is to co-ordinate activities of resources so as to reach the defined goals.

Three facets of the managerial job:-

As pointed out by *Peter F. Drucker*, the manager performs three types of work simultaneously –

1) Managing a business.

2) Managing managers.

3) Managing workers and work.

Almost every decision or section a manager tasks affect all these facets.

Management a Business:-

Management a business is the task pertaining to the economic performance of the enterprise and requires the supply of goods and services at acceptable prices. To be effectives, a manager must be a creator rather than a creature of the economy. Secondly, managing managers is necessary for making a productive organization out of human and material resources. It involves co-ordination of efforts and function of managerial personnel, setting goals for them and directing their activities. Finally managing workers and work is concerned with organizing and directing employees and their work. It calls for the evaluation of the workers both as a human being and as a resource.

Principles of Universality of Management:-

Management is in everywhere, along with same methods, same technique. In the words of *Frederick W. Taylor*, "The fundamental principals of scientific management are applicable to all human activities from our simplest individual acts to the work of our great corporations."

Universality of managerial principals also means that they are transferable. They are transferable from one department to another department regardless of the nature of the function in the other department. For example, a sales manager may be promoted as the General Manager the General Manager of a printing press may be successful in managing a cotton textile concern, the captain of a Cricket team may become a Competent Supervisor in a factory and so on. Not only that, the Universality of managerial principals also means that they can be transferred from one level to another level. All managers perform the same managerial functions regardless of their position in the managerial hierarchy.

Chapter – 7

Evaluation of Management Thought

Vrwick and **Brech** have written about contributions of thirteen pioneers in, 'The making of Scientific Management'. The pioneers have been drawn from various parts of the world, Six from America, Three from France, Three from England and One from Germany. As might be expected, the list of contributors cannot be made exhaustive. There are many research scholars and social thinkers who have enriched our knowledge of management science. In recent years; Management movement has acquired a new dimension from the 1950's through the contribution of several disciplines. As **Haynes** and **Massie** point out, there are at present Six streams of thought that have influenced the scientific management, Viz, 1) Quantitative approaches 2) Managerial economics and accounting 3) Universal of Management 4) Scientific Management 5) Human relations and 6) Behavioral Science.

Current management thinking is characterized by the system approach to management and the contingency view of organization. These two approaches call for a refinement extension and synthesis of both past and present contributions. These approaches will continue to be the key to effective management in the 1980's both the approaches accept the dynamics and complexities in organization structures.

Management in Antiquity:-

Among the human being there is co-ordination, while living one has to directing and co-operate to others and therefore it can be said that management has a equally long history. Although the 20th century is marked in history as the area of scientific management. The recent emphasis should not create the impression that it is the phenomenon of this century alone as attempts at solving management problems date back into antiquity. In earlier days management generally took the form of personal leadership. In ancient Mesopotamia there was a group of Priests who did management work. They directed and governed by virtue of their authority as representative of the gods whom the people worshipped.

Egypt & China:-

Interpretations of early Egyptian papyri, extending as for back as 1300 B.C. indicates the recognition of the importance of organization and administration in the bureaucratic states of antiquity. Similar records exist for ancient China. Confusion's parable includes practical suggestions for proper public administrations to choose honest, unselfish and capable public officers.

Greece:-

Although the records of early Greece do not give much insight into the principle of management. The very of the Athenian commonwealth with its councils popular courts, administrative officials and board of generals indicates an appreciation of the managerial function. Socrates' definition of management as a skill separate from technical knowledge and experience is remarkably close to current understanding of the managerial function. In the discourse with Nicoma chides Socrates is reported to have made the following observations on management, "I say that over whatever a man may preside, he will, if he knows what he needs and is able provide it, be a good president, whatever he has the direction of a chorus a family, a city or an army...... is it not also duty...... to appoint fitting persons to fulfill the various duties......? To punish the bad, and to honour the good...... Do not, therefore Nicoma chides, despise men skillful in managing a household for the conduct of private affairs differs from that of public concerns only in magnitude.

The Bible:-

Moses says the book of Exodus in the Bible, chose able men out of all Israel and made them heads over the people, rulers of thousands, hundreds, fifties and tens and they judged at all seasons the hard causes they brought up to Moses but every small matter they judged themselves, this contains the foundation of some principals like selection of competent personnel, delegation of authority and the exception to the rule which have proved highly beneficial in large enterprises.

Ancient Rome:-

The record of management in ancient Rome is incomplete, although it is well known that the complexity of the administrative job evoked considerable development of management techniques. The existence of the Roman magistrates with their functional areas of authority and degree of importance indicates a scalar relationship characteristic of organization. Indeed, it is thought that the real gejus of the Romans and the secret of success of the

Roman Empire lay in their ability to organize. Through the use of the scalar principle and delegation of authority, the city of Rome was expanded to an empire with an efficiency of organization never before observed.

Impact of Industrial Revolution on Management:-

The evolution of management concepts runs almost parallel to the evolution of manufacturing processes. With the advent of the industrial Revolution some time in the middle of the eighteenth century, machines were designed to increase productivity and remove many of the laborious workers were not chained to or dominated by, their inefficient hand tools, instead the workers were provided with equipment with which they could substitute machine power for muscle power. Since much of the machinery was massive, stationary and dependent on a given source of power, such as a waterfall, it was necessary to locate materials and equipment in a central plant. Employees went to their work instead of receiving it, as in the putting-out system. And so the factory system, as it is known today, became a dominant feature of the economy. Under this system land (including buildings) hired labor, and capital (supplied by owners) are made available to the entrepreneurs, who strives to combine these factors in the efficient achievement of a particular goal.

The Advent of Scientific Management:-

The new scientific management emphasized rational decisions rather than decisions based on tradition.

The scientific method can briefly be summarized as follows.

1) Recognize the problem, analyze it and define objectives.

2) Gather and analyze the necessary data.

3) Synthesizes possible alternatives.

4) Review and evaluate each alternative.

5) Test conclusions, if possible.

6) Take selected action.

7) Review results and, if necessary, correct action.

8) Formulate and test principals based on experimental results of many cases.

In the words of L.F. Urwiek, "Modern management has thrown open a new branch of human knowledge, a fresh universe of discourse."

The beginning of scientific Epoch in management:-

The real being of a science of management did not occur until the last decades of the nineteenth century. A group of remarkable persons in the united states, Mstly engineering-Frederick Taylor, Hennery Lawrence Gantt, Harrington Emerson, Cart Barth, Frank Bunker Gilbreth, Lillian Moller Gilbreth , and others must be credited with lying the foundation of a management movement which, in due time, became known as 'Scientific Management'. Introduction of mass production large-scale industry and the use of expensive machinery resulted in difficulties of maintaining harmonious relations between the employer and employees. This projected to the fore front the importance of utilizing adequate methods and principals in solving problems of management. This epoch in the history of management will be remembered as an era in which traditional ways of managing were challenged, past management experience was scientifically systematized and principals of management were distilled and propagated. This has been characterized as an era of a new movement of scientific management in the sense that new ideas and approaches were taking roots and a body of management principles and philosophy was emerging from the efforts of many who were directed with business administration and management the contributions of the pioneers of this age have a profound impact in furthering the management known-how and enriching the store of management principals. In the history of management thought, the following literature deserves special mention.

Date	Author	Book Title or Paper.
A.D. 1903	F.W. Taylor	Shop Management.
A.D. 1906	F.W. Taylor	On the Art of Cutting Metals.
A.D. 1909	H. Emerson	Efficiency.
A.D. 1910	H.L. Gantt	Work, Wages & Profit.
A.D. 1911	H. Emerson	Twelve Principles of Efficiency.
A.D. 1911	F.W. Taylor	Principles of Scientific Management.
A.D. 1916	H.L. Gantt	Industrial Leadership.

A.D. 1919	H.L. Gantt	Organization for Work.
A.D. 1919	The Gilbreths	Applied Motion Study.

During the brief period, 1903-1919 the teachings of these four great leaders in industry were given to their American contemporaries and so to the world.

> ➢ **Nineteenth Century Contributions:-**

During the period following the industrial revolution, certain pioneers tried to challenge the traditional character of management by introducing new ideas and approaches. Notable contributions of this period are as below-

♦ **Professor Charles Babbage (U.K. 1729-1871):-**

He was a Professor of Mathematics at Cambridge University and suggested the use of accurate data, obtained through rigid investigation, in the management of an undertaking. *Herbert N. Casson* in his book 'Creative Thinkers' (1931) writes that, " Babbage found by visiting many factories in England and France that many manufactures were wholly unscientific – the most of their work was guesswork. He found to his great surprise that factories were run by traditional and that they relied upon opinions instead of investigations and accurate knowledge. Babbage felt that the method of science and mathematics could be applied to the operation of factories; and invented a calculating machine called 'The Differential Engine'. In his writings which include an essay 'On the Economy of Machines and Manufactures'

43

(1832). He urged the management of an enterprise, on the basis of accurate data obtained through rigid investigation the desirability of finding out the number of times each operation is repeated each hour the dividing of work into mental and physical efforts, the determining of the precise cost for every process and the paying of a bonus to the workers in proportion to his own efficiency and the success of the enterprise.

♦ **James Watt and Mathew Robinson Boulton:-**

James Watt Junior (1796-1848) and Mathew Robinson Boulton were the sons of the distinguished inventors of steam engine. They used the following management technique in their engineering factory at sono.

1) Market research and foresting.
2) Planned machine layout to facilitate better flow of work.
3) Production Planning.
4) Maintenance of advanced control reports and cost accounting data and procedures.
5) Standardization of components and parts.
6) Elaborate statically records.
7) Provision of welfare of personnel with sickness benefit scheme administered by an elected committee of employees.
8) Scheme for developing executives.

♦ Robert Owen (U. K. 1771-1858):-

Robert Owen managed a group of textile Mills in Lanmark (Scotland) from 1800 to 1828, and is well-known as The Promoter of cooperative and trade union movements in England. Hardly any industrialist was interested in his workers welfare on-the-job and off-the-job during those days, but Robert Owen firmly believed that workers performances was influenced by the total environment of working conditions and just treatment. He introduced new ideas of human relations – shorter working hours, housing facilities, training of workers in hygiene, education of their children's, provision of canteen, rest places, sops and so on – at a time when longer hours, employment of children and conditions of work were the order of the day. Though his approach was paternalistic, his methods would entitle him to be known as the Forerunner of Personnel Management.

◆ Henry Robinson Towne (U. S. 1844-1924):-

Henry Robinson Towne, president of the famous lock manufacturing Company 'Yale and Towne' took particular interest in the better management of the concern and applied his own ideas successfully to his factory. He was also the president of the American Society of Mechanical Engineers in 1889, in a paper captioned, 'The Engineer as an Economist', presented to the Society annual conference in 1886, he urged the combination of engineers and economists as industrial Managers. This combination of qualities, together with at least some skill as an accountant is essential to the successful management of industrial works. Towne was interested in organized exchange of experience among managers and pledged for an organized effort to pool the great fund of accumulated knowledge in the art of workshop management.

◆ Clade Henri Saint Simon:-

He was one of those effective thinkers who adumbrated the philosophical, economic and social system in which the role of

45

capital is constructive, creative and entrepreneurial rather than of exploiting the resources for its own benefit. This concept took concrete shape through the establishment of the famous Parisian bank named 'Credit Mobilier'. This bank became an important determinant of industrial growth by channeling the liquid resources of France into creative developmental activities. Saint Simon's model of development bank is still followed by underdeveloped countries for the improvement of their national economies.

♦ Tylors Philosophy in the scientific Method:-

However, it is only since the advent of Frederick W. Taylor with his famous work, 'The principles of Scientific Management' published in 1911, that greater attention has been paid to scientific management as a separate discipline worth studying. According him, the duties of management were –

1) To develop a science for each element of a man's work.

2) To select scientifically and train the worker instead of allowing him to train himself.

3) To Co-operate with the workers to ensure that the scientific principles were adopted in the works; and

4) To divide responsibility between management from the workers who resisted time study procedures and standardization of every aspect of their performance. They rebelled against being treated like machines. Therefore he formulated his philosophy in a set of three essentials or principles –

1) The substitution of a science for the individual judgment of the workman.

2) The scientific selection and development of the workman, each man has been studied, taught and trained and one may say experimented with instead of allowing the workmen to select (the work) themselves and develop in a haphazard way.

3) The intimate co-operation of the management with the workmen, so that thay together do the work in accordance with the scientific laws which have been developed instead of leaving the solution of each problem in the hands of the individual workman.

♦ Gantt's Philosophy of Humanity in Industry:-

Gantt was also one of the earliest pioneers in the scientific management group in the United States, his major interest being directed to the human being in industry. He considered the human element as the most important one in all problems of management. He is also described as, "The Forerunner of modern industrial democracy". He is of course popularly known by one particular chart which bears his name although he evolved many charts. His important appeal was that wider recognition should be given to the human factor in management and that the financial incentive is only one among many of the motives which influence men.

♦ Emerson's Philosophy of efficiency:-

According to Emerson, "Efficiency means that the eight things are done in the right manner, by the right men, at the right place, in the right time. True efficiency means ameliorating conditions, for the workers, both individually and collectively not only for the worker, but also for the employer- not only for the employer but also for the corporation, and finally, for the nation".

47

He called his philosophy the Gospel of Efficiency. So that he quoted, "Efficiency dose not consist in extreme effort, but in the elimination of undesirable effort and waste of all kinds, the elimination of child and woman labor in competitive employment. Efficiency does not come to increase the nervous strain of the age which gives railroad spine to the locomotive engineer, and results in premature exhaustion of the Telephone girl, but it come to palliate that strain by standardizing both effort and reward. It comes to determine justly and without reference to wage rate, the standard time of any operation, and to guarantee to each worker, whether low or right, a special reward in proportion to individual efficiency.

Gillbreth's Philosophy of the one best way (U.S. 1868-1924):-

Gilbreth's distinctive contribution was to develop 'Motion Study' as a primary tool for managers. He also emphasized human effort and devised methods for showing up wasteful and unproductive movements. He maintained that there is one best way to perform an operation or do a piece of work in industry. This teaching may appear to be a doctrine of unattainable perfection. Rather it is a statement of the philosophy of the engineering standard. He proved the truth of his theory being a builder himself by simplifying the motion used in hourly number of bricks laid from 175 to 350. thus increasing productivity one hundred per cent over the previous system. He was the first to apply the motion picture camera to record and analyses performance. He was the also the first to classify the elements of human motion of 'Therbligs'. He and his wife Lillian Moller Gillbreth maintained that for an organization to hold its members it must consider, apart from the welfare of the organization, the welfare also of the individuals comprising that organization.

Chapter – 8
Schools of Management Theory

The mental philosophy of the manager will automatically be conditioned by his own thinking and frame of reference. His learning will automatically be in favors of a certain philosophy or school of thought. The various schools of management thought with have grown up in management circles.

1) The Classical School:-

After duration of industrial revolution product system developed and business automatically spread. That's why we had to accept many methods of management. New thinking we had to accept. Lots of thinkers had put the own thinking in front of management in the end of nineteenth century. That is called classical theory or school. Basically in these thinkers– F.W. Telloyer, Henry Fayol, Vrwick, Max Weber, were involved in it.

2) Management Process School:-

This group suggests, Management as a way of accomplishing things thoug organized groups. In practice this means –

1) Analyzing process.
2) Establishing a conceptual framework for process.
3) Identifying principles underlying the process.

This approach builds a theory of management and looks at government. The process remains the same but the environment of management theory is seen as a way of summarizing and organizing experience, so that practice can be improved.

This school of thought, often referred as the 'Traditional' School was founded by Henry Fayol. Later innovations included Fredrick W. Taylor.

Basically, modern proponents of this school look at the functions of the manager.

1) Planning

2) Organizing

3) Staffing

4) Directing

5) Controlling.

It was become management process.

3) Scientific Management School:-

Frederick Winslow Taylor (1856-1915) well known as the founder of the science management movement was the first to recognize and emphasis the need for adopting machinist in Philadelphia, U.S.A. Taylor rose to be the chief engineer at the Midvale Engineering works and later on served with the Bethlehem works, where he experimented with his ideas and made the contribution to the management theory for which he is so well known. Taylor tried to diagnose the causes of low efficiency is due in the lack of order and system in the methods of management. He found that the management was usually ignorant of the amount of work that could be done by a worker in a day as also the best method of doing the job. As a result, it remained largely at the merely of the workers who deliberately shirked work. He therefore, suggested that those responsible for management should achieving higher efficiency. The scientific method consists essentially of-

1) Observation

2) Measurement

3) Experimentation

4) Inference

Taylor and Associates and followers perfected efficiency techniques through which these principles could be implemented. The main elements of Scientific Management are –

1) Work study involving work measurement and work improvement through scientifically conducted Time and Motion studies, Methods studies and Fatigue studies.

2) Standardization of tools and equipment for workmen, machine speeds and working conditions.

3) Scientific selection, Placement and Training of workers by a Centralized Personnel Department.

4) Introduction of functional organization.

   (Separating the functions of planning and implementation between two sets foremen.)

5) Mental Revolution on the part of the employers and the workers in regard to the mutual Co-operation for increased productivity and also about the introduction of the scientific method in management.

4) The Human Relations School *OR* The Human Behavior School:-

This approach has been called the 'humanreations', 'Leadership', or 'Behavioral Science Approach'. Because this approach to analyzing management is based upon the fact that managing involves getting things done through people; there fore, management must be centered on inter-personal relations.

In this school the stress is on the 'People' part of management and the understanding aspects of this relationship. The range of this thought in this school goes from –

(a) Human relations and how the manager can understand and use this understanding.

(b) The manager as a leader and how he should lead.

(c) A study group dynamics and interpersonal relationships.

While human behavior is a heavy factor in management, it would be difficult to accept many of this school as management theories although they explain many aspects of management behavior.

Human relations school also called as a Neo Classical Theory. In this school Elton Mayo, Mack Greger, Maslow is involved.

Main Functions:-

1) Organization is a social process.

2) Employee in organization are comes together to social and moral need.

3) Co-ordinate relation establish with staff.

4) To look at the workers as human view point.

5) Participating of employee in management.

6) To establish infortncy organization.

7) Formal relation & informal relation.

5) The Contingency Theory / School:-

It is called as situation approach system. It is direct related to Situation. There can't be forever managerial action in the management. It may be –

1) Accident.

2) Natural disaster.

3) Fire.

   With the along above situation management has to charge in its planning, organization, controlling. This is changeable theory in management.

Characteristics:-

1) To go through situation.

2) Manager has to different work in different situation.

3) Management system relates to situation.

4) Manager has to use of his principles as per the situation.

5) Management has not control in future.

Chapter – 9
Social Responsibilities of Business

The need for greater professionalization is emphasized in the modern context by the stress on the manager's social responsibilities context by the stress on the manager's social responsibilities and not judging him merely on the basis of profit or profitability. As *professor Dasgupta* apply points out that, "Whether in public or the private sector, every enterprise must be so conducted that it can serve its own objectives as well as social purpose". According to him this social responsibility was not fixed and had always to be related to the pressures at a particular point of time current pressures. According to him, are as follows, namely –

1) To remove or to reduce the quantum or centralized authority.

2) To make all positions accessible to persons who have the qualities.

3) To remove authoritarian attitude by top management in relation to employees.

4) To provide opportunities to all employees for growth and advancement through participation in management problems.

5) To use modern technology and science in business for the development of innovational personnel.

6) To create additional jobs each year for absorbing young trained persons.

7) To help government in increasing the rate of economic growth.

The Beneficiaries

Action of the manager at fact society for example misleading advertising can hurt the consumers. Personnel bias and philosophies can result subordinates it is managements responsibility to use most productively the limited resources in terms of material and human beings made available to the enterprise. In India, in the context of the socialistic pattern of society, these obligations increase in importance. These responsibilities can basically be divided in terms of four 'publics' or groups of people or beneficiaries namely-

1) The owners or shareholders of a company.
2) The employees.
3) The customers and consumers.
4) The community at large.

(1) Responsibility towards Owners :-

It is top management's basic responsibility to ensure that the resources available are used for the benefit of the owners or shareholders in a company. The managers are using the properties of the owners and are in a position of trust to them. They thus own honesty and dedication to the interest of the owners for example, the Chief Executive must be good judgment in how he influences the Board of Directors the Board's decisions and polices fairly honestly to his subordinates. The owner's look upon the Chief Executive and the Board of Directors to produce profits and pay them reasonable dividends out of such profit as well as protect their investment. The dividend is the return legitimately expected by shareholders on their investment. The safe and wise use of stability and security of the management the shareholder is likely to gain in the form of capital appreciation or increase in the market price of his shares. It is thus management's responsibility to the owners to ensure that the organization is strengthened and grows adequately in the interests of the owners.

(2) Responsibility Towards the Employees :-

The employees are important members of the company or organization contribution their mite to the success of the enterprise. Abuse of the employees in the past has led to the labor legislation and trade unions. Co-operation and harmonious relations between the managers and the workers can alone ensure maximum productivity of the organization. The responsibilities to employees should not be looked upon within the narrow limits of legal specifications. They must be viewed in the large-context of social responsibilities to the employees as well as responsibility for greater productivity of the enterprise. It is management's responsibility to provide adequate monetary and psychological rewards as wells as appropriate job security. In the Indian context, where job opportunities are scarce and the unemployment problem has raised its ugly head, responsibility for job security is the greater. Apart from providing reasonable job security, selection of employees must be made fairly and without discrimination on the ground of caste, community or sex. Emphasis must consisitently be on suitable educational qualifications and merit in terms of possible effectiveness on the job for which selected. Existing employees should be encouraged to develop themselves with future education where necessary so that they may be ready for future promotions. In fact, today's responsibilities extend even to providing such educational opportunities and job training to the employees at the company's expense. In addition, a fair and reasonable wage or salary must be paid in terms of the effort required of the employees. Increasing payments should result from improved productivity or performance. Besides, the working conditions should be pleasant and safe. Adequate information should be supplied to the employees so that they feel as if they are a part of the organization or members of a team directing their efforts to be attainment of certain overall goals. These are some of the social responsibilities owed by the managers to the workers or their subordinate employees.

(3) Responsibility Towards Consumers / Customers :-

The modern outlook based on the marketing concepts is for organization to be consumer-oriented. Its objectives are to identify needs which can be converted into products or services of the company, aimed at satisfying such consumer needs. Particularly in the context of the prevailing seller's market in many commodities in India, it is the social responsibility of the management to ensure that the consumers are provides adequate quality products at reasonable prices. To this should be added prompt, courteous and dependable service. Constant effort should be made to improve the products and services offered to the consumers. Recognition of such responsibility has resulted in emergence of organization in India such as 'The Fair Trade Practices Association' established to promote a code of fair trade practices and set up effective machinery for its enforcement. If the customer is constantly harassed with exorbitant prices, the result is likely to be Government price control legislation.

(4) Responsibility Towards Community :-

Organization's also a responsibility towards the community at large. Many factories are located in and around village which supply the labor force. Thus these factories must assume a central and important role in the life and activities in India have already started village improvement schemes.

Management by Objectives (MBO)

Today the expression 'Management by Objective' (MBO) becomes popular in view of the advantages. It is sometimes also described as 'Results Management' or 'Management by results'. It is aimed at increasing the effectiveness of managers by placing the responsibility on each manager for achieving results for his part of the organization's activities. Thus objectives are set by each manager either with participation or consultation or through the 'Top-down approach'. Where the subordinate concerned is actively associated in formulating his own objectives or goals in the light of the broader departmental or overall company objectives, he is more likely to achieve such goals or objectives as he has participated in the decision-making process. Whatever the method used the following are some of the essentials-

(1) The individual and departmental objectives must dovetail into the overall organizational objectives. The individual and departmental objectives are divided, so that they may integrate into achievement of the overall organizational objectives.

(2) Objectives must be clearly defined and communicated. For example, the statement that, "The objective of advertising is to increase the sale of product" is not explicit or sufficiently defined. Is the objective merely to increase the sale? If so, by what per cent? A clearer objective would also speak in terms of increasing awareness of a certain percentage of a particular market segment.

(3) Objectives and goals must be reasonably attainable. If goals objectives or standards are fixed to high, the result would be frustration and from the beginning a decision by the individual concerned not to try and achieve the impossible.

(4) Objectives fixed for an individual must onsider factors uncontrollable by the individual which might affect the achievement of the individual goals.

(5) Objective should be reviewed periodically for the necessary changes.

The Nature of Objectives

Objectives being part of the planning are concerned with the future or attainments at some future period in time. They may be –

(1) Immediate or short-term objectives.

(2) In the distant future or long-range objectives.

They may be general overall objectives or specific objectives in each area such as production, marketing and so on. A managerial objective is defined be Terry as, "The intended goal which prescribes definite scope and suggests direction to efforts of a manager". It enables the physical and mental work to be directed towards some goal or purpose and thus stimulates action in the desired direction.

Advantage of Management by Objectives

(1) They provide a basis for planning and for development of other types of plans such as policies, budgets and procedures.

(2) They result in a better appreciation of what the organization is attempting to achieve, and five meaning and direction to the people working in the organization.

(3) They help coordinated behavior of the various groups in the organization so that all the groups pull in the same direction as the objectives are duly established and communicated.

(4) They constitute standards for the control of the organization and the human effort.

(5) They provide a motivation device by giving proper direction to the workers who are thus motivated to direct to their energies towards constructive ends.

(6) They give direction and force management to think ahead as to process of having to establish objectives- short-term and long-term forces those in charge of accomplishing to look ahead, plan for eventualities and take a course of action which will help the organization or department concerned towards the right path for future success.

Some Concepts of Objectives

If a businessman is asked what the objective of his business is, the answer would probably be 'Profits'. If further asked, "What is your business?" he may answer, "To manufacture and sell books", if he is a publisher of books or "To manufacture iron and steel", if he is in charge of an iron and steel company. Are these correct descriptions of overall nature of the business?

(1) The Growth Objective:-

According to some managers, a business has to run to stand still, managing that constant effort at growth are required even to maintain the existing situation. This is more so in a buyer's or competitive market environment. Adequate growth provides opportunities for promotion to the employees. It increases the strength of the company for survival in competition as with growth and larger scale of production it is in a position to offer its products at lower prices. Thus management must be clear regarding the growth objective or the size objectives which can also harrowed down in terms of the Geographical area of operation which may be national or international.

(2) The profit Objective:-

We are concerned with profit, as the true measure of our performance that we have maintained the organization in sound financial condition and have obtained for the shareholder a proper return on his investment representing a fair reward for the contribution made. But we are also concerned with the well-being of the organization in its totality as we believe that industry is an organ of society specifically charged economic advance through making resources productive that economic progress can be made into a powerful driving force for human betterment social justice.

Increasing Productivity Objective

Allied to the profit objective is the productivity objective, the word 'Productivity' having more favorable image than the word 'profit'? Besides, recent year have shown increasing interest by organizations in increasing productivity of orations; particularly in the light of price control and the desire to lower costs. Take the example of A.C.C. Ltd. in the 1950's such activities were intensified and by 1963 a separate division called productivity division was even formed its objectives was –

(1) To secure optimum utilization of the available re-source for higher operational efficiency.

(2) To plan and organize better working method on the shop floor and in the offices.

(3) To analyses various other aspects like substation of imported machinery and spares by indigenous ones, in plant standardization, cost control, inventory control and product development. This division is divided into several department such as –

(i) Industrial Engineering.

(ii) Inventory Control.

(iii) O.R. & S.Q.C.

(iv) Cost & Statistics.

(v) Technical Audit & Quality control.

(vi) E.D.P.

The formation of this division is particularly important in the light of the several constraints placed on the industry such as price control, restriction on distribution and difficulties of securing wagons for transportation. Besides, as in other industries, cost seems to be spiraling with increases in excise duties, railway freight, and dearness allowance and so on. Thus with shrinking margins of profit, it becomes more essential for organizations in such industries to become cost conscious and productivity minded.

Social Obligations Objectives

A social obligation is an important part of business. These obligations extend to supplying adequate products at reasonable return on investment to shareholders and so on. However, frowning on profit, in this context is erroneous. Unless a business unit makes sufficient profits now can it pay adequate dividend to its shareholders or provide continuous research and development with a view to improve its products for its consumers or customers? Unless sufficient income is generated how can the organization continuously increase the wages and salaries of its employees? It is only when reasonable profits are made, that an organization in this sense can fulfill its social obligations. Thus profits constitute one measure of a business unit's efficiency. For example, it would be better if public sector undertakings provided products and services at reasonable prices and ended up in a small surplus rather than proudly claimed, as some do, of making, "A loss in the public of inefficiency and has to be born by someone, generally, the tax payer in the ultimate analysis, in the case of the public sector. Some public sector undertakings are showing a profit because they are efficient. An organization which makes a loss will have more difficulty in convincing an outsider of its contributions to society.

Specific Objectives

Specific objectives must be evolved in each area such as marketing, productions and so on. For example, the following type of questions will have to be answered to evolve such specific objectives, namely –

(1) What is the nature of the gods or services to be produced by the company?

(2) What is the extent of diversification into different groups of products to be manufactured desired by the organization?

(3) What is the extent of Geographical market to be covered i.e., will it be local. National or international?

(4) What is the type of the company's customers, i.e., whether consuming public industry or Government or a combination?

This type of question will have to be answered to arrive at more specific objectives. For example in the area of marketing apart from the overall marketing objectives regarding –

(1) The nature of the business.

(2) The extent of diversifications.

(3) The minimum return desired on investment.

Specific objectives will have to be evolved in the area of product, pricing, distribution and promotion. In the light of the market segment to be aimed at –

(1) The types of products to be manufactured will have to be decided.

(2) Pricing objectives will have to be established,

(3) The extent and type distribution required will have to be determined which would depend on the nature of control desired.

(4) More specific objectives in connection with advertising will have to be established with regarded to creating consumer and dealer awareness, creating a favorable image and encouraging immediate sales.

These specific objectives then must dovetail, or be integrated into the overall company objectives.

Multiplicity objectives

Thus there is s large variety of business objectives. Drucker sets eight areas in which objectives of performance and result have to be set, namely –

(1) Market standing.

(2) Innovation.

(3) Productivity.

(4) Physical and financial resources.

(5) Profitability.

(6) Manager performance & development.

(7) Workers performance and attitude.

(8) Public responsibility.

There might be, as **Drucker** points out real protest against the inclusion of the last three intangibles. The proper selection and blending of appropriate objectives can alone set the business ship on the right course of continued profitable growth and increased contribution to society.

In short the M.B.O. process namely into five phases or sequence.

(1) Finding the objective.

(2) Setting the objective.

(3) Validating the objective.

(4) Implementing the objective.

(5) Controlling and reporting status of the objective.

Areas of Social Obligation

Social obligation relates to our culture. One has to observe the social obligation, which will be increase the states of our country and build up our culture.

1) Environment Planning:-

We live in Environment. While living in present there are lot of pollution, water pollution, land pollution and air pollution. Most of all air pollution created by vehicles and industries. There are two immediate effects of air pollution; climatic changes and toxicity. Both of which may endanger life. During winter season the smoke is a menace in Mumbai, Colcata, Durgapur, Baroda, Chennai, and Delhi.

In all the cities Co_2 and So_2 content has been significantly increasing in recent years. Water pollution is equally insidious practically all around the world and particularly in the industrialized Nations where large and small bodies of water are found. Posing potential health hazard to people, pure and natural water is becoming increasingly scare. A major contributor to water pollution is sewage from cities. Future among the enemies, one that is most insidious, disquieting and dangerous is noise which menaces a large number of humanity now living as member of industrial urban civilization. Increasing urbanization is adding fuel to fire. One poisonous by- product of modern technologies is pandemonium, which is becoming painfully louder each year and it may drive cacophonous urban dwellers to a permanent silence. It is within the social responsibilities of management to uproot lock and barrel, air, water and noise pollution.

2) **Utilization and Conservation of National Resources:-**

The first and the foremost social obligation of management is to efficiently utilize and conserve the national resources in general and the resources of the concern in particular. Any relaxation in this regard may be deemed as 'Social-sin'. Society is keenly interested in the rational utilization of its resources and survival of its business institutions and it is the obligation of management to support and indicate society's interest in this respect.

3) **Social obligation towards four group in society:-**

   (i)   The owners of the business to whom it has to guarantee a fair return on the capital invested by them.

   (ii) The customers who have to be satisfied about the quality, price, etc. of product.

   (iii) The employees, each of whom must be contended and encouraged to contribute his best to the joint endeavor.

   (iv) Society at large of which it must promote the general good. There is a great deal of tug-of-war of tension in the interest of these diverse groups. The primary responsibility of management is to reduce the areas of such conflict and to bring about harmony of interest among diverse groups.

4) **To work within the framework of the laws of the land:-**

Another set of social obligations of management of to observe the rules of the competitive game strictly, to work within the framework of the laws of the land; as land down by the Government and to support the socio-economic development policies of the government.

5) Social Health and Family Planning:-

Problems of technological unemployment, problem of squalor, congestion, housing and crime in urban areas in which business firms are located, problems of population and family planning, problems of depletion and degeneration of natural and other resource which organization use. Problems of deleterious effects of industrial products (like DDT, patricides and even chemical fertilizers) on human health and environmental balance- all these to fall within the orbit of social responsibility of management.

Recommendations for Environmental Planning:-

Some Recommendations in short

(1) **Towards society:** - We have lot of population. That is why we can not maintain the population for this (i) Government should be taken immediate decision to control the balance of population. (ii) We must be given awareness of to the society about population. (iii) To create awareness of 'Hum do Hmare do'.

(2) **Towards conservation:** - Conservation of forest, conservation of animal, conservation of water, land, rivers, streets, etc. To maintain balance of nature. Industrialist should have awareness of above conservation. For this- (i) Government should be given some rules and regulation to maintain the conservation.

(3) Towards Education: - Education gives the information of balance of environment. Because environment relates to the people, if the people are creates them no one can protect the environment. For create good awareness education programmers have to be undertaken through television, radio, film, schools, college, new papers, university. Such type of education can give the proper understanding to the people.

Government Role

Government has such type of department which implement the rules and regulation for people –

(1) Government should have strict legislations along with industrialist, company, to control all farms of populations-air, water, noise etc.

The municipal corporation should have a long-range plan in the respect of settlements and sustain industrial development.

(2) Department of Environment Ministry:-This department should have a master plan for the total urban sustainable development which would emphasize scientific and aesthetic environment planning.

(Sustainable = such type of development that there should not be over development which will be harmful the society and should not be wear development, which will be harmful to the society. In short –

Sustain – Balance

Sustain – Progress withought loss and only prosperity).

www.ingramcontent.com/pod-product-compliance
Lightning Source LLC
Chambersburg PA
CBHW081220170526
45165CB00009B/2883